LIVING MASTERS OF MUSIC—II.
EDITED BY ROSA NEWMARCH

SIR EDWARD ELGAR

EDWARD ELGAR IN 1900

(From a photograph by Russell & Sons)

SIR EDWARD ELGAR

BY ROBERT J. BUCKLEY

JOHN LANE: THE BODLEY HEAD
LONDON & NEW YORK.   MDCCCCV

Printed by BALLANTYNE, HANSON & Co.
London & Edinburgh

CONTENTS

ILLUSTRATIONS

vii

SIR EDWARD ELGAR

"Self-taught I sing. 'Tis heaven and heaven alone,
Inspires my song with music all its own."

ODYSSEY.

"The heights by great men reached and kept,
    Were not attained by sudden flight,
But they, while their companions slept,
    Were toiling upward in the night."

INTRODUCTION

DURING a conversation with Dr. Frederick Temple, Archbishop of Canterbury, allusion was made to certain anecdotes concerning him. In his brusque, explosive way he ejaculated :

" All lies !"

The same might be said of many anecdotes of Edward Elgar, and here is the point I wish to make.

Whatever this book states as fact may be accepted as such.

The sayings of Elgar are recorded in the actual words addressed directly to the writer, and upon these I rely to give to the book an interest it would not otherwise possess.

As to the critical opinions submitted in these pages, I will only say that they rest on a close study of Elgar's works, extending over nine or ten years. *Quot homines, tot sententiæ.*

I have not given any space to consideration

of Elgar's wanderings from the paths of contrapuntal rectitude, as laid down by the theory
formalists. The Roman soldiers tied weights
to their sandals when marching for exercise,
that by discarding them in time of war they
might rejoice in comparative lightness and
freedom. So, it would seem, are musicians
weighted in the study of strict counterpoint,
that in free composition they may derive addi-
tional inspiration from the joy of casting the
load aside. It may be suggested that Elgar
has cast away not only the weights but also
the sandals. The sequence of consecutive
fifths in "The Apostles" is calculated to make
the old theorists uneasy in their graves. But
this is only history repeating itself. The Man
of Progress is necessarily the Breaker of
Laws, and if the Law-breaker is justified by
results, we can demand no more. The rules of
art are for the Novice, not for the Master, who,
however, cannot be a Master without a novi-
tiate under strict rule.

In der Beschränkung zeigt sich erst der Meister,
Und das Gesetz nur kann ihm Freiheit geben.

My thanks are due to Sir Edward Elgar for

the copy of his early form-study; and to Mr. Hubert A. Leicester, of Worcester, for the quintet portrait and other illustrations.

It is perhaps needful to add that the body of the book was not only written but also printed before the well-earned honour of knighthood was conferred on its subject.

ROBERT J. BUCKLEY.

MOSELEY, WORCESTERSHIRE,
July 14, 1904.

Ich habe mich
vergessen
Home on Mon-
day, ... them!

Ed: Elgar

I

EARLY YEARS

EDWARD WILLIAM ELGAR was born at Broad-heath, near Worcester, June 2, 1857. His surname, of Scandinavian origin, is a modernised form of Aelfgar, or "fairy spear." He is the eldest surviving son of W. H. Elgar, a native of Dover, and Ann Greening, of a yeoman stock hailing from Weston, in Herefordshire, and he is therefore apparently as English as can be. The elder Elgar left Dover to become an assistant in the music publishing house of Messrs. Coventry and Hollier, then in Dean Street, Soho, London, where, amongst other musical experiences, he used to hear Dragonetti play the pedal part of Bach's organ fugues on the double-bass, Barnett, who brought out an arrangement for piano and bass, taking the piano. Domenico Dragonetti, prince of contra-bassists, died in 1846. Five years before this date, W. H. Elgar settled in Worcester, became organist of the Roman Catholic Church of Saint George, a position he was destined to hold for thirty-seven years, and in partnership with his brother established a music warehouse and made his influence felt in the musical doings of the city. It was at his suggestion that the masses of Cherubini in D minor and Hummel in E flat were first heard at the Three Choir meetings, and whenever the Festival took place at Worcester he played amongst the violins. A busy, striving man, this elder Elgar, doing all that in him lay to secure a fitting allowance of the bread that perisheth, not without endeavour after the artistic side of life. An accomplished musician, the father of the future composer discerned in the youthful Edward certain premonitions of unusual talent. The boy was considered clever ; but means were narrow, and the parents were not of those who sacrifice the rest of the family for the sake of one, however promising. Thus it was that Edward Elgar enjoyed no exceptional opportunities, no unusual privileges. At an early age he was sent to a ladies' school, where he took elementary pianoforte lessons, between which slight instruction and the hints on violin technique he received from a Mr. Frederick Spray there was a great gulf fixed. No teacher took him over systematic courses of scales and studies ; no learned mentor supervised his exercises in harmony, counterpoint, canon and fugue. He heard no lectures on musical form, received no practical hints on orchestration. From the five-finger exercises of the ladies' school to the lessons of Mr. Spray stretched a desert arid of regular musical instruction. The most impressionable years of life were passed without the stamp of any teacher's personality. The boy was left to grow as he chose—musically ; to take any and every artistic impression that might be floating in the air ; to form himself on any model that might capture his young fancy, or to remain formless, at his own good will and pleasure. About him was no vestige of the prodigy, or rather none that the undiscerning world could see. Wherein is no wonder. For while the multitude are quick to recognise and applaud the musical acrobat, it takes something like genius to detect the earliest signs of superior intellectual or creative force.

Since the organist of the Church of Saint George had not leisure to give special attention to the musical education of his family, and since there seemed no sufficient reason why Edward should be singled out for instruction, the boy was in this respect largely left to his own devices. And here was visible the first development of the phenomenal tenacity, the indomitable perseverance, which characterise the Edward Elgar of a later day. Relying on himself he discovered for himself, invented his own methods, evolved his own strategy of learning, losing precious time in cutting his path through the solid rock, yet gaining immeasurably in force of character ; toiling by circuitous paths when short cuts, unknown, lay on every hand ; ever thinking strenuously, on the watch for smallest hints, developing the tiniest germ of knowledge into larger and still larger proportions ; an idealist, dreaming ; a toiler, working ;—a compound of Keltic fire and fancy, derived from some remote unknown ancestor, and the cold, stern determination of the practical Anglo-Saxon ; baffled here, victorious there ; every achievement a new point of departure, every summit painfully gained

displaying a wider prospect ; the very obstacles
in his path arousing a keener spirit of combat,
a deeper resolution to emerge a conqueror.
Not that he cherished the smallest ambition of
fame. An inborn inextinguishable thirst for
knowledge spurred him on. Instinctively he
felt that the highest order of pleasure was the
discovery of truth, listening to the teaching of
truth, and the adoption of its teaching. A pile
of old books in the loft of a stable were to
him as pearls of great price. His mother was
a reader of good books. The greatest poets
were known to her, and through her to the
family. This middle-class woman of com-
pulsory economies, and with seven children to
look after, had affinity with the best English
literature ; moreover, she read translations of
the Latin classics, of the Greek tragedians, and
talked in the home of what she read. " The
best woman that ever drew breath " is the
description of one who knew her for a life-
time, and this testimony of a non-relative is
confirmed on every hand. Blessed are they
who have mothers like the mother of Edward
Elgar ! The bent of the parent explains the
bent of the son. His boyish choice of books

from the stable loft is no longer inexplicable.
There were the "Arcadia" of Sir Philip
Sydney, Baker's "Chronicles," Drayton's
"Polyolbion," and other volumes regarded by
the shy, retiring youth as treasures of un-
speakable worth. Without his musical sur-
roundings Edward Elgar might have been a
poet, might have emulated Dante or Milton.
He was born to high emprise. His turn of
thought inclined to the serious, the heroic, the
epic. For him there was fascination in all
things beautiful. He had a love for every
form of art. Certain mediæval carvings in
Worcester Cathedral moved him strangely ;
the soul of the artist of centuries ago evoking
corresponding vibrations in the artist-soul of
the boy. Across the ages spirit spoke to
spirit.

Though without formal instruction, the
future revolutioniser of oratorio was not without certain demonstrable advantages. Music
and musical instruments were available : their
use was not forbidden ; moreover, the boy
could sit at the organ with his father, drinking
in the music of Mozart and Haydn and the
older composers who have written for the ser-

vices of the Church of Rome. A born student,
an omnivorous reader, he cared little for boyish
sports. His mind was occupied with higher
thoughts. Absorbed by his enthusiasms,
other things seemed small. Cricket had no
chance against counterpoint. Edward Elgar
was possessed by an intense desire to make all
knowledge his province, his early environments
directing him to music as a speciality. Urged
by enthusiasm, silent but unquenchable, he
laboured incessantly in season and out of
season, teaching himself the violin, the viola,
the violoncello, the piano, the organ, the
bassoon : in short, any and every instrument
that came within reach. A constant stream
of music passed through the warehouse. He
studied it all, especially prizing that of the
great masters. To him a Sonata of Beethoven
was as clusters of grapes in the vineyards of
Eshcol, and a Bach prelude and fugue more to
be desired than much fine gold. His love of
music was admitted, his industry admired.
But love of art and its fervent pursuit are not
always tokens of original talent, and the sleepy
city of Worcester remained unconscious of the
genius that in a few years was to make the

ancient town famous wherever good music was heard.

Meanwhile Edward Elgar attended school at Littleton House, where a Mr. Francis Reeve, who supervised the education of some twenty-five to thirty boys, appears to have made a lasting impression on the future composer, who told the writer that to those far-away days was due his oratorio "The Apostles." He said :

"The idea of the work originated in this way. Mr. Reeve addressing his pupils, once remarked : 'The Apostles were poor men, young men, at the time of their calling; perhaps before the descent of the Holy Ghost not cleverer than some of you here.' This set me thinking, and the oratorio of 1903 is the result." A moment later he added, with characteristic luxury of humour too deep for smiles, "I do not remember more than twenty-seven fellow pupils, but there must have been three or four hundred, as that number (or thereabouts) are kind enough to remind me of our early acquaintance at Littleton House."

In addition to the combined influences of the private school, the organ-loft, and the

LITTLETON HOUSE, NEAR WORCESTER, WHERE EDWARD ELGAR WENT TO SCHOOL

music warehouse, must surely be added those
which emanated from the manifold romantic
and historic associations of the city itself.
There was the Guildhall with its statue of King
Charles and its cannon left on the fateful field
of Worcester, "The Faithful City." There
was the cathedral with the mysterious crypt
where good Bishop Wulstan worshipped in the
days of the Conqueror, perhaps religiously
resentful of the raid of Hardicanute, who set fire
to its predecessor just twenty-five years before
the Conquest. Then the church held royal
memories, though not precisely of the sort that
smell sweet and blossom in the dust. King
John attended Mass under its roof in 1207, and
sleeps his last sleep below the gilded effigy in
the choir. It may be that the future writer of
a Coronation Ode admired King John as some-
what of a champion in the matter of crownings.
As a pious Roman Catholic, the youthful
Elgar may have approved of his four corona-
tions, and especially of that in which the
harassed King accepted the crown from a
legate of the Pope, and agreed to hold the
kingdoms of England and Ireland as a papal
tenant, paying a thousand marks a year.

The young dreamer was constantly in the cathedral, listening to the anthems and services of the old English masters, noting everything, making endless inquiries, prosecuting an interminable research. Very early his sensitive mind was attracted by the infrequent chromatic harmonies occurring in this kind of music. Did a chord strike him as more than usually effective or expressive, he would not rest until he had studied its environments, the disposition of the voices, and whatsoever else gave beauty above its sister chords. This leaning to chromatics, be it observed, was by the musical light and leading of the time accounted rank heresy, if not flat blasphemy. The critics were severe on all things not diatonic. Young composers were exhorted to rely, not on "portentous harmonies intended to be dramatically expressive," but on "the glorious resources of contrapuntal device." Music was to be constructed on scientific lines, and none was good unless sicklied o'er with the pale cast of thought. Musicians were fettered by the theories of Fux and Albrechtsberger and Cherubini just as earlier the scientists had been fettered—in

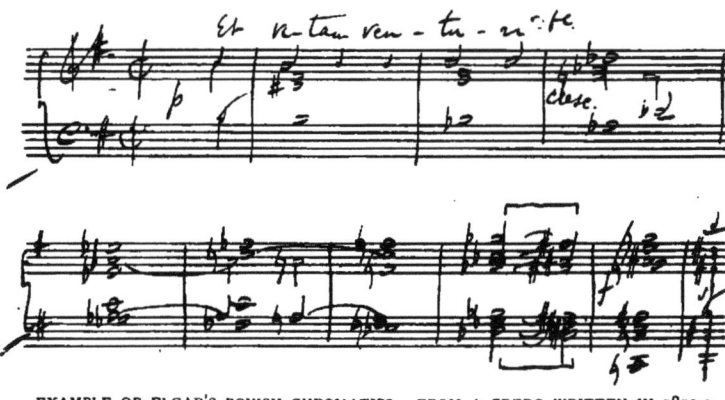

EXAMPLE OF ELGAR'S METHOD OF STUDY. THE REMARKS IN THIS AND THE
PRECEDING EXAMPLE, WITH THE MUSIC, ARE FAC-SIMILES OF
ELGAR'S HAND IN 1904

EXAMPLE OF ELGAR'S BOYISH CHROMATICS, FROM A CREDO WRITTEN IN 1872-3

geology, by the hypothesis of catastrophes; in chemistry, by the hypothesis of vital forces. That the composing of music was subject to iron rules was made clear by the examination papers of the Universities of Oxford and Cambridge, ancient repositories of golden knowledge, unique plenipotentiaries of the muse, and chartered conferrers of immortality. In those wonderful sheets the aspirant to musical honours, his eye in fine frenzy rolling, saw oratorio in the rough. There was the crude material from the like of which Bach and Handel had evolved their colossal choruses. Your course as a candidate was perfectly clear. You took your *canto fermo* and on it built several species, and several cunning mixtures of species, of strict counterpoint. You took your fugal theme, and having decided to treat it tonally or otherwise, a vital point, you wrote your exposition, your episodes, your stretto and your pedal, by no means forgetting your augmentation and your diminution, and particularly remembering that while consecutive fifths meant relegation to the darkest depths of Tartarus, no university professor could resist the magic of a

canon cancrizans, say in the Hypomixolydian
mode.

Such in large measure was the orthodox
musical atmosphere of England when Edward
Elgar, still a child, was penetrated with the
charm of certain sudden transitions in the
masses of Mozart and the symphonies of
Beethoven, the latter only available to him in
pianoforte arrangements. The story of every
mind susceptible to artistic feeling affords
instances of sudden impressions of far-reaching
influence. One of the earliest and most powerful of these came upon Edward Elgar on his
first reading of Beethoven's First Symphony.
Only the pianoforte score, but the effect was
there. It came upon him like a lightning
flash. The transition to the key of D flat, and
back to C, in the minuetto, left him breathless—
" sank into his very soul "—convinced him that
counterpoint was not the last word of musical
art ; that Tallis and Byrd and Orlando
Gibbons and the rest of the classic church-
composers had not exhausted the possibilities :
that, despite the dicta of the critics and
university professors, the " solid diatonic
style " did not represent the Ultima Thule of

composition; and, finally, that Mozart and Beethoven, having attained the highest plane of emotional expressiveness, were the best models for study. Already, unaided and alone, he pored over an old copy of Catel's "Treatise on Harmony," translated by Mary Cowden Clarke. Then he had Mozart's "Succinct Thorough Bass," translated by Sabilla Novello, "a dear old book" still cherished among his treasures. "Cherubini on Counterpoint" was eagerly devoured, and preludes and fugues innumerable flowed from his ever-busy pen. Already the creative instinct was strong within him, and he wrote incessantly. "The worst of the old text-books," he says, "is that they teach building but not architecture." Later he owed advancement to Stainer's book on Harmony, which, at the time of its publication, the old school of organists regarded askance as radical, revolutionary, tending to "red ruin and the breaking up of laws," and still later found invaluable hints in Sir Hubert Parry's articles in Grove's "Dictionary of Music."

In the music-warehouse, in the organ-loft, in the lumber-room of the stable, the art-spirit of

Edward Elgar was developing. All men who have risen head and shoulders above their fellows have been dreamers in their youth. But while they dreamed their fill, they combined their capacity for seeing visions with an infinite capacity for work.

II

YOUTH AND MANHOOD

AT fifteen Edward Elgar left school, and at the instance of a legal friend of the family entered a solicitor's office with the object of becoming a lawyer, versed in the quillets and quiddets of the English code, and possibly not altogether without an eye on the woolsack, a peerage, and a final termination in the odour of sanctity and the House of Lords. From June 1872 to June 1873 the budding composer held a steady Coke-and-Blackstone course, after which he quietly told his parents that all was not precisely as he could wish, and that he would prefer to make himself generally useful about the warehouse and the church. Once more he became saturated with an atmosphere of music. He sat with his father at the organ and extemporised introductory voluntaries. He would frequently accompany the services. He

was always at work. He plodded through the
"Organ Schools" of Rink and Best without
assistance ; continued his study of theory ; con-
ceived a plan of study at Leipzig, and began to
learn German ; played much of the pianoforte
music of Kotzeluch, Schobert and Emanuel
Bach ; wrote fugues and other forms of music,
abandoning his original fancy for scoring his
compositions on four lines instead of five
(touching concession to the conventions of an
artificial age), kept up his practice on various
instruments, with an especial leaning to the
violin ; played the bassoon in a wind-instru-
ment quintet, consisting of two flutes, oboe,
clarinet and bassoon, for which weird associa-
tion he wrote endless music, of which he now
speaks as "no good, on account of the unusual
combination," and in due course was admitted
as a violinist to the orchestra of the Worcester
Festival Choral Society, conducted by Mr.
Done, organist of the cathedral, and to other
orchestras in the Worcester district, ultimately
attaining local fame as a solo performer on his
favourite instrument.

Another element in Elgar's education was
the Worcester Glee Club, which dated from

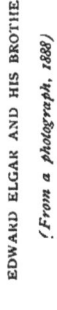

EDWARD ELGAR AND HIS BROTHER

(From a photograph, 1888)

THE WOOD-WIND QUINTET PARTY

W. B. LEICESTER   EDWARD ELGAR   H. H. LEICESTER
(Clarinet)   *(Bassoon; Composer)*   *(First Flute; Director)*

F. EXTON   F. T. ELGAR
(Second Flute)   *(Hautboy)*

1810, and which was a well-known and highly
appreciated feature of the musical life of the
Faithful City. Week by week during the
winter months, amateurs and cathedral singers
met for mutual enjoyment, singing the fine
music of the older English masters. The programme generally consisted of ten numbers,
eight glees and two songs, the proceedings
being invariably commenced with " Glorious
Apollo," after which the smoking of pipes was
in order; not with the puny briars of these
degenerate days, but with antique Broseley
" churchwardens," whose length suggested a
dignified aloofness, and whose curling incense
gave a glory to the scene.

The music was not exclusively vocal. There
were instrumental nights, when the best per-
formers of Worcester appeared in their best
form. Among these was Edward Elgar's
father, who could hold his own as second
violin, or in case of need accompany the songs,
and make himself generally useful, as well as
agreeable. There was a good deal of Corelli ;
Haydn's symphonies were apparently inex-
haustible, and the overtures to Handel's
oratorios suited the conservative tastes of the

B

music-lovers of the staid cathedral town. The
conductor of the Worcester Festival Choral
Society had no patience with what was called
the modern school, and the "preposterous
compositions" of Schumann were by him
doomed to an eternal and merciful oblivion.
Naturally the city took its tone from the cathedral organist, whose geniality was the theme of
general praise, and whose capacity for playing
from the old vocal scores, and at a pinch from
a figured bass, had earned for him the reputation of abysmal profundity.

W. H. Elgar joined the club about 1843,
Edward Elgar coming about thirty years
later, to play with the violins. By this time
the Handel overtures were thought old-
fashioned. A spirit of revolution was abroad,
or if not of absolute revolution, a spirit of
progressiveness. Instead of the overtures to
"Saul" and "Samson" and "Esther" and
the "Occasional" oratorio, all of which had
been prime favourites twenty to fifty years
before, there were overtures by Mozart,
Rossini, Auber, Vincent Wallace, Bellini, Balfe
and Bishop. The glees and madrigals of contemporary composers were added to the club's

répertoire, and innovation went so far as to introduce German part-songs. To all this varied music did the observant Edward seriously incline. For two years he was the chief accompanist, receiving great commendation, from which he shrank as undeserved. He was a violinist, he said, not a pianist, " and for that matter anybody could play accompaniments." But the local cognoscenti thought differently, and even recognised in him an instinct for supporting and making the most of the vocalist, as well as in pulling him through when threatened by accident, or when "slightly below his usual excellent form." At the same time some of the older men were wont to declare that Master Edward was prone to put more into the music than had occurred to the composer, and that in certain cases his varied harmonies had not only startled conservative auditors, but had made the singer nervous.

When the Society began to print its programmes, it was felt that a great advance had been made, though there were not wanting sticklers for the good old times, who shook their heads and whispered one another in the ear, and prophesied upon it dangerously. In 1879 Edward Elgar was appointed pianist and conductor. Years before that an accidental absence of the leading violinist of a Worcester amateur society had given him a chance, and having shown his ability, he was promoted to the post of leader. In January 1878, he was presented with a violin bow in thankful remembrance of his services, which bow remains in his study to the present day, along with his trombone, his favourite picture of Beethoven, his scores of the masters, his choice copy of the *Spectator*, and his infinite variety of treasure.

The Worcester Glee Society was kind to the young musician. The name of Edward Elgar often appeared on the composer's side of the programme, his compositions showing a decided versatility. He wrote for the glee party, for the band, for the solo singers, for anything and everything, for anybody and everybody. In season and out of season he jotted down his musical thoughts whenever they occurred. And they were always occurring. All things were clothed in imaginary music. Every personality was represented by a musical expression,

FAC-SIMILE OF THE OPENING OF A BARITONE SOLO WITH ORGAN ACCOMPANIMENT
COMPOSED BY ELGAR WHEN A BOY, FOR THE SERVICE OF ST. GEORGE'S
ROMAN CATHOLIC CHURCH, WORCESTER

which came unbidden and unsought. The preludes and fugues, the glees and songs, the music for the wood-wind quintet were succeeded or accompanied by quadrilles and other light music written for the band of the Worcester County Lunatic Asylum, of which the composer became conductor at the age of twenty-two. One day in each week was spent at this institution, where he coached the band in the proper manipulation of their instruments, and when he had taught them to play, conducted performances which were designed to alleviate the condition of the patients, the *personnel* of the band being derived from the attendants. Again the composer had to adapt himself to unusual conditions. There was a flute, a clarinet, first and second cornets, euphonium, bombardon, double-bass, first and second violins, and piano with occasional additions and emendations. It was hard to write music to fit this extraordinary combination ; but it was done, and the Asylum Board, not unmindful of the claims of art, commissioned original quadrilles, and at the day of reckoning ambled in with five shillings per set. Thus, in defiance of the proverb, was the

prophet honoured in his own country. At
this period Elgar was scoring Christy Minstrel
songs at eighteen-pence each, and sitting up
all night to copy music that would have cost
him three and sixpence in coin of the realm.

Speaking of his early violinist days, he says,
"When a child, I once came in wrong with
a second violin passage. I shall never forget
my horror. I feel it even now. I did not
analyse my sensations at the time, but I know
that it was an artistic horror."

While he worked in the secular world he
worked in the field of sacred art. Motets,
masses, all kinds of church music flowed from
him in a ceaseless stream. New music for
special occasions was always forthcoming
from the unofficial assistant organist, who as a
boy not over well supplied with pocket money,
was wont to |bargain with his schoolfellow,
Hubert A. Leicester, for organ-blowing ; Elgar
to pay by playing certain specified pieces, after
which he played to please himself. Hubert A.
Leicester was director of the boys' wood-wind
band for which Elgar wrote many of his
earliest compositions.

III

MANHOOD AND MARRIAGE

FROM the age of fifteen Elgar maintained himself; and at twenty, having some notion of becoming a solo violinist, he went to London and took five lessons from Adolf Pollitzer, who ran him over his scales, showing the fingering of three octaves, these being the days of Baillot, before Schradieck appeared. The teacher also gave five pieces of music by way of solatium, and was surprised to find Elgar not only remembering the unmarked fingering, but also playing the five pieces from memory. The student continued to visit Pollitzer at intervals for some years, but in the end was not satisfied with himself. He recognised that time had been lost, and moreover the solo-violinist notion had begun to pall. The question arose, What course to take? Would he go on with the violin, or with the piano, or settle down as

an organist ? He took time to consider, and
while he pondered he worked. *Laborare est
orare.* His visions of study at Leipzig had faded
into nothingness through want of funds. But
he was economical, and on the last days of
1882 contrived to visit Leipzig for a holiday,
and by no means " to study German methods,"
as has been asserted in print. His first hour
brought a comic incident. On the stroke of
midnight Elgar entered a hotel where a waiter,
mistaking him for a New Year guest, ushered
the astonished traveller into the thick of a
private party standing on chairs, wearing paper
caps of wonderful shapes and colours, and at
the precise moment raising their glasses with
shouts of " Prosit Neu-jahr ! " Among this
throng of revellers, Elgar, with his travelling-
cap, overcoat and umbrella, must have looked
like a New Year Santa Klaus. He bowed and
fled without looking behind him. His first
adventure at the Gewandhaus concerts brought
another touch of humour. He wished to hear
Schumann, then regarded as terribly advanced,
and altogether too radical for the provincial
orchestras of England, and if not Schumann
some other revolutionary. " As I climbed the

ST. GEORGE'S ROMAN CATHOLIC CHURCH, WORCESTER, WHERE EDWARD ELGAR WAS ORGANIST

stairs, a little late (an exceptional thing with me), I heard a familiar strain. I was surprised and paused. Yes, it was—it was—the andante of Haydn's Surprise Symphony! There was, however, some Schumann, the Overture and Scherzo in E minor, a fine work, though the opening reminds me of Cherubini's overture to 'The Water-carrier,' not thematically, but in the pattern."

Three years after this Elgar succeeded his father as organist of Saint George's, Worcester, and looked like settling down as an obscure provincial teacher. He continued to play the violin in orchestras, kept up his composition practice, and gave lessons. In 1889 he married the daughter of Major-General Sir Henry G. Roberts, K.C.B., a lady of musical and literary skill, who fully appreciates her husband's artistic significance; the world's indebtedness to her influence and encouragement will assuredly be made known at a future day. There is one child of the marriage, a daughter. In the same year Elgar resigned his position as organist, and went to live in London, principally with the object of hearing good music. This was the beginning

of his real opportunity. As a boy he had written
for orchestras which he had never heard, and
had gloried in the casual visits to the provinces
of the Haigh-Dyer Opera Company, which gave
" Norma," "La Traviata," "L'Elisire d' Amore,"
and other well-known operas. As a young
man without means for help in study and
without skilled advice he had played in all the
orchestras available, at the last desk, if necessary, in order to gain experience. When he
heard a sonorous passage or one that sounded
thin, he would score the piece from the band
parts, counting the bars and painfully ascer-
taining for himself why the passage had that
particular effect. He had no book on Musical
Form, and being struck with the symmetry of
Mozart's G minor symphony, he barred out a
full score and wrote and orchestrated a
complete G minor symphony of his own,
modulating where Mozart modulated, not
slavishly, but following the master's lines with
reverential closeness. To extend the catalogue
of his strivings is needless. For surely enough
has been said to remind the aspirant of Buffon's
" capacity for infinite pains," and to convince
him that Edward Elgar deserved success if

OPENING OF ELGAR'S SYMPHONY WRITTEN IN 1878, AS A FORM-STUDY AFTER
MOZART'S IN G MINOR, COMPOSED IN 1788

he had never achieved it. While living in London he worked incessantly, running down to the midlands once a week to give lessons. In 1891 he went to reside permanently at Malvern, eight miles from Worcester ; in 1893 the " Black Knight " was produced in his native city ; and in 1896 his " Lux Christi," produced at the Worcester Festival of the Three Choirs, heralded the dawn of a new period of oratorio. In the same year came " King Olaf ; " and in 1897 the " Te Deum " and " Benedictus " were produced at the Hereford Festival. The " Enigma " variations, and " Caractacus," the latter written for the Leeds Festival of 1899, and the " Sea Pictures " produced at the Norwich Festival, showed versatility, while in 1900 " The Dream of Gerontius," produced at Birmingham, attracted the attention of Julius Buths, who translated the libretto, and in December 1901 gave a performance of the work at Düsseldorf, with a success that led to a repetition at the Lower Rhine Festival of May 1902. In 1900 the University of Cambridge had conferred on the composer the honorary degree of Doctor in Music, amid universal approval and felicitation. Elgar was forty-three. If ever musician showed tenacity Elgar was the man. Few indeed are found who, without teachers, and in the face of suppression, have the courage to toil on with upward eye and never-failing heart for thirty years. The inclusion of his name in the list of birthday honours of 1904 did honour to the list, and from that moment "Sir Edward" instead of the clumsier "Dr." Elgar became a household word. His career is as remarkable for its patient tenacity as for its genius. It was at Hereford, in 1903, that he said to the writer, in quiet casual response : "Yes, I sometimes think that if I had not been rather persevering, I should never have done anything at all." With which all who know will remain in hearty accord.

IV

EDWARD ELGAR AT HOME

IT was in the "Black Knight" period that I first visited the composer at "Forli," a charming cottage under the shadow of the Malvern Hills, meet situation for the dreamy tone-poet, the creator of ravishing harmonies. It was the riotous summer. The hedge of the lawn before the house was in flower, and the wicket opened amid poetic blooms. Close at hand was a larger lawn, a pleasaunce of sloping banks and smooth-shaven turf, whereon was a sunny tent, the opening of which commanded a glorious valley, extending to the purple horizon. "Forty miles and never a brick!" ejaculated mine host, as we took our seats in this ideal retreat, where were easy chairs, a table and a couch which reminded me of Rossini dashing off operas in bed. There, too, was a proof copy of "Lux Christi," afterwards called "The Light

of Life," concerning which we held sweet con-
verse together. The Worcester Festival was
due in a few months, and the composer felt
that much depended on the success of this, his
first choral work to be heard at an important
meeting. Overflowing with enthusiasm, he
spoke rapidly and continuously of the state of
musical art in England, deploring the fate of
works commissioned for festivals, which, after
painstaking and elaborate production, were
heard no more. His bearing was that of one
in deadly earnest, not wholly inaccessible to
the jocular, but too intent on his aim to waste
time on anything not directly leading to the
goal. He laughed but rarely, and his mirth
was soon checked. In the heat of the early
struggle, and with the winning-post in sight,
his mind seemed occupied with a fixed resolve
to make the world aware of the power he
believed to be his own. "King Olaf" was in
hand, and the tent was littered with sheets of
music-paper bearing myriad pencil marks, un-
decipherable to the stranger as the hierogly-
phics on a blackbird's egg, and, like the pro-
verbial lost pocket-book, of no use to any one but
the owner. From the tent-pole a flag fluttered

in the breeze, delicate hint that the composer
was at work, and must not be lightly disturbed.
But, as he explained, the restriction was more
in jest than in earnest, and the flag was frequently struck.

Of a fugue in " The Light of Life " he said :
" I thought a fugue would be expected of me.
The British public would hardly tolerate
oratorio without fugue. So I tried to give
them one.   Not a 'barn-door' fugue, but
one with an independent accompaniment.
There's a bit of canon, too, and in short, I
hope there's enough counterpoint to give the
real British religious respectability ! "   All this
of course in badinage.   Questioned as to his
actual feeling for the perpetuation of the fugal
style, he rose and walked rapidly about, as is
his custom when interested.   " It has been
done," he said.   " Bach has done it.   No man
has a greater reverence for Bach than I.   I
play three or four preludes and fugues from
the ' Well-tempered Klavier every day.'   No. 33,
in E major, is one of my favourites.   No. 31
is another, and No. 29, a wonderful masterpiece, is constantly before me.   But my vene-
ration for Bach is no reason why I should

imitate Bach. I certainly can't beat Bach in
the Bach manner, and if any one asks me why
I don't write in the Bach style, I think I shall
say, 'It has been done, once and for ever—
by Bach ! You were talking of contrapuntal
rules and restrictions. I have gone over them
all : marked, learned, and inwardly digested
everything available in theoretical instruction
I could come across (and I think I have come
across most of what has been written) ; and I
cherish a profound respect for the old theorists.
They were useful in their day, but they were
not entitled to lay down hard and fast rules for
all composers to the end of time."

He paused and walked out into the sunshine.

" My idea," he continued, "is that there
is music in the air, music all around us,
the world is full of it and—(here he raised
his hands, and made a rapid gesture of capture)
—and—you—simply—simply—take as much as
you require !"

Truly a short compendium of the bookish
theorick, and as satisfactory as short, the only
important objection being occasional absence
of the Elgarian grip.

Not music only, but books and literature,

came under review on this occasion. The composer revealed himself as a book enthusiast, a haunter of the remoter shelves of the second-hand shops, with a leaning to the rich and rare. In the sitting-room was a grand piano, in the study a smaller instrument, surrounded by books, and books, and more books. He declared himself a devoted reader of all kinds of literature, and chuckled over a novel wherein an orchestra was described as awaiting the fall of the conductor's bâton, the trumpeters with their instruments pressed to their lips in eager anticipation, the piece being the introduction to the " Messiah " overture. Referring to his leaning to the *leit-motiv*, he said that his early studies in this direction were based on Mendelssohn, long before he had seen or heard a note of Wagner. His sketch-books of twenty years before contain experiments in all kinds of curious rhythms, 5-4, 7-4, 15-4, and even 11-4, of which the only published result seems to be the 7-4 " Lament " in " Caractacus."

It was during this visit that Elgar spoke of a Malvern book club, a sort of literary federation, of which he was the first member, which enabled Malvern readers to know each other's

C

libraries, the late Mrs. Lynn Linton being an enthusiastic supporter. The surrounding piles of books were expressive of the man, but other features of the study spoke his many-sidedness. A large portrait of Wagner was conspicuous, and a board over the fireplace displayed in poker-work an ascending flash of chromatic semi-quavers. "The Fire-motive," he said, "from the 'Ring of the Nibelungen'; one of my own attempts at decoration." A cosy room, with quaint bric-a-brac from foreign lands; bits of carving from the Bavarian Highlands, then his annual summer resort. He showed the silver buttons of his waistcoat as specimens of Bavarian handicraft, described the character of the people, and pointing to the score of the "Light of Life" said he wrote the beginning of number three recitative and chorus, "As Jesus passed by," six thousand feet above the sea-level.

"It has at least that claim to be called high art," he remarked airily.

Tacked lightly to the wall was an uproarious illustrated joke cut from a German newspaper, and in a dim corner a photograph of a thirteenth-century panel sculpture of the Crucifixion from

Worcester Cathedral. "It shows a wonderful feeling," he remarked, as he looked upon it lovingly. Presently he spoke of recreations, and declared a liking for golf, remarking that if not of the first force he was certainly animated by the best intentions. He was for some time a follower of the American craze for kite-flying, with its aerial photography and its scientific aims, desiring to invent a compensating kite that should adapt itself to whatsoever currents it might meet in its celestial course. Kites, it seemed, were not to be relied on in unexpected emergencies. Sailing away in a suitable wind, and giving promise of irreproachable conduct, they were apt suddenly to jib, to fly in the wrong direction, to bolt, kick, plunge, buck, cavort, and to be guilty of other deplorable excesses. It was his hope to restrain these unregenerate tendencies, to break in and bridle the innate *diablerie* of the fiery untamed kite in a state of nature, and by taking much thought to compose a kite that might be useful. Nothing came of it except the fall of his neighbour's spouting, and the occasional employment of a powerful navvy to pull down the rebellious thing from the central blue.

Looking at Elgar's music, one may see in its general audacity the spirit of one who would invent a flying-machine. "Eripuit cœlo fulmen" may surely be said of him. But if he has snatched fire from heaven, the feat was not accomplished by means of "long-tailed," or "square-tailed," or "bob-tailed" kites.

In these pleasant days at "Forli," he declared his musical creed to be a love of everything that was good, whatever its style or period. He would go a hundred miles to hear a Wagner opera, and would enjoy a Haydn quartette, if a good example. Music, he thought, should be progressive ; to stand still was to perish, or at least to degenerate. He would have enjoyed working on opera, but wanted both subject and libretto. Such was Edward Elgar three months before the production of "The Light of Life."

V

EDWARD ELGAR TO-DAY

"You are prone to imagine there are several Dr. Elgars, according to the clothes and the circumstances in which you see him. There is one in evening dress pacing the corridor of a concert-room, in which a conductor is taking Elgarian works at unauthorised tempi. There is another in rough tweed and leggings, who frequents unfrequented lanes with chosen friends, who, armed with a spirit lamp and other impedimenta, take tea under hedges 'like tramps.' A third, wearing an elaborate waistcoat, smokes genially in front of his own poker-work 'fire-music,' burnt on the panel over the study grate. A fourth walks slowly along the Worcester High Street, buried in a battered Panama pulled down to his chin. A fifth, attired in the customary suit of solemn black, ambulates *lento*, as though weary, in the precincts of a cathedral during a Three Choir Festival. This one wears a tall silk hat, crushed down on the forehead, and gives the impression of a distinguished colonel home for a year's holiday, and at present attending a funeral. Dr. Elgar is tall, spare, angular, grave and courteous. He will listen with attention to skilled comment on his work, but gives short shrift to aggressive incompetence. Shadowy legends exist of patronising persons who were made to regret the indestructibility of matter, and to wish themselves well out of the Cosmos."

This description, written by me for a London journal in October 1903, though in jocular vein, has been accepted by many good Elgarians, and on this account may be allowed to stand. There are also several Dr. Elgars of mood, and to describe these would indeed be a delicate task. There is the Dr. Elgar of few words and preoccupied manner; one who gives the uninitiated the impression of unearthly solemnity. At the other extreme is the brilliant and cultured talker, running over with enthusiasm, full of ideas about all things in heaven and earth, and with clear-cut

opinions he is not afraid to express.   There is
also the good listener, who will give ear to the
opinions of others on music, and on his own
music, with what looks like abnormal patience
and humility.   "All I require," he says, "is
that they shall know something about it."
He is a dramatic *raconteur*, and his description of an unseen band heard at a seaside
resort in Italy was something memorable.
Intensely humorous were the "peep, peep" of
the clarinets, the "pom, pom" of the trom-
bones, and above all the unwritten rush of the
bass trombone from tonic to dominant by
means of the chromatic scale.   Dr. Elgar is
not a great laugher in point of cachinnation.
He laughs internally, deeply, silently.   Still he
laughs out occasionally, though seldom.   His
laugh is not melodious.   Rather is it harmonic,
a dissonance, a sort of minor-second that is
never resolved.   The one laugh specially
noted was, however, a benevolent laugh, be-
stowed on one who had told a story for
which it was clear that he expected a laugh.
And Elgar laid the sacrifice on the shrine of
friendship.

 His new home, Craeg Lea (which name conceals an anagram), three miles from the old, is just so much nearer to the "Caractacus" hill. Some other things have changed since the "Lux Christi" period, though little or no change is seen in Elgar himself. A significant addition to the drawing-room ornamentation is the big wreath given after "Gerontius" at Dusseldorf. Nowadays he speaks not all of the future but of the past, of "Gerontius" at Sheffield, at Hanley, at Hereford, at Manchester. Drifting into general conversation he thinks musicians need good education. More culture is desirable for vocalists. Too many depend on their voices and a popular repertory. He regrets worship of mere technique, and declares that the uncultured violinist plays without convincing, whatever his technical skill. And human experience is needed. To hear the cleverest youth play a great concerto is like hearing a boy preacher. There is no authority. Yes, education is needed by musicians, and outdoor life. His own love of the open air is owing to his having as a boy lived at Broadheath, three miles from Worcester, which meant constant walking to and fro. Golf is a grand game, because you

can't think of anything else when playing.
Bicycling is good ; did thirty miles the other
day, and was stopped by the snow. During
railway journeys amuses himself with crypto-
grams ; solved one by John Holt Schooling
who defied the world to unravel his mystery.
Led back to music, he takes the trombone and
plays a little, to exemplify what can be written
with good effect, and presently wandering to
books, suggests that if people would index
good books instead of writing music, there
would be some sense in it. As to his ideals, he
would like to see a permanent opera in England,
and for his personal fancy would like to write
all the music he feels without being called upon
to superintend its production. He expresses
a strong desire to know everything about
everything, from an iron foundry to a printing
machine, and episodically dilates on the pond
aquarium in the drawing-room, describing the
habits of its queer inmates, occasionally stimulating their enthusiasm with a long spoon, by
means of which he handles them as if he loved
them. There is a fellow who rolls himself
up in moss and leaves and pretends he is not
there, and another who sports a green jacket

and poses as a bit of leaf. There are fresh-
water shrimps and snails and tadpoles, in
which he seems to take as much interest as in
oratorio. His talk is presto scherzando, and
while he talks he stands or walks about, that
as interest increases at any point he may get at
his audience effectively. But for his pipe he
would lack repose ; the pipe saves the situation. He has been accused of a cold and
scathing sarcasm, but this would depend on
the subject and the constitution of the listener.
When rehearsing a choir who were tamely
giving a chorus on " The Sword" in " Caractacus," he said, " You appear to be singing of
putting up an umbrella." His nervous sensibility may sometimes place him at a disadvantage, but those who best know him speak in
praise of his large-hearted sympathy and
desire to help where help is needed. Miss
Marie Hall told the writer how much she owed
to Edward Elgar, who took her up when she
was nine, and gave her lessons at his home, a
fact strangely ignored by Miss Hall's bio-
graphers. When the blind musician, William
Wolstenholme, composed his degree exercise,
it was Edward Elgar who committed the work

to paper from the composer's dictation, devoting many afternoons to this laborious, self-imposed task. Then he went to Oxford with his friend to act as his amanuensis in the examination room. Teaching was not always agreeable to Edward Elgar. "To teach the right pupils was a pleasure," he once said; "but teaching in general was to me like turning a grindstone with a dislocated shoulder."

VI

THE PROGRESS OF ELGAR

A REVIEW of Elgar's published works impresses
by the musicianship and finish which mark the
earliest ; the absence of clearly traceable influence ; the general sense of beauty ; the
growing individuality and gradually increasing
importance combined with proportionate depth
and complexity. There are, of course, certain
fluctuations in point of æsthetic quality. Beethoven did not always write on the level of the
Fifth Symphony, and Elgar is not always at his
best.   But there is nothing trivial, nothing un-
worthy a serious musician. The "Ave Verum"
of Op. 1 looks like a boyish work with a bar or
two of the "Gerontius" period at the close, the
only hint of Elgar-character in the motet,
which is graceful, smooth-flowing, and normal,
if not commonplace enough to be popular.   It
was in 1885 that Mr. William Cole Stockley, of

Birmingham, thought a piece in the Mauresque style, since published as Op. 10, good enough for production at one of his orchestral concerts, this being Elgar's first appearance as a composer outside Worcester. So far the prestige of the Three Choir meetings had been denied to him, save as a performer among the violins, but his compatriots at last, on the unmistakable verdict of others, accorded him a chance at the Worcester Festival of 1890, when his overture " Froissart" was produced, title and conception being due to a speech of Claverhouse in " Old Mortality." Looking over the score of this first overture, one marvels that recognition was deferred for years. Its vigour, invention, scoring are far above the average hack-work of festival productions. " Froissart" has the true fire, the undeniable magic of inspiration. True, Joseph Bennett told Elgar to " go on," but he was practically alone. If the critics had known enough, or if knowing enough they had dared, they might have paraphrased what Macaulay said of Milton's " Ode on the Morning of Christ's Nativity," namely, that any one stanza was enough to prove that a great genius was born to the world. Yet the " Times " could

only laugh at Elgar for using the double-
bassoon. The Twelve Organ Voluntaries,
Op. 14, sold to a publisher for five pounds,
showed a certain something above and beyond
mere cleverness, while the "Chanson de Matin"
and "Chanson de Nuit," published later, might
have made the composer's name popular as a
writer of acceptable small things. But "Froissart" was a bid for something higher, and a
successful bid, though most of the critics
accorded nothing more than the regulation
"safety" commendation. Opus 20, a String
Serenade for orchestra, is of surpassing love-
liness. Its beauty is of Schubertian intensity,
though of different character. Only a master
could have written this gem-like piece, which
incidentally exemplifies Elgar's perfect adapt-
ability to the means proposed. The Serenade is
for strings, not only nominally, but in its very
essence. Scored for full orchestra, the piece
would lose its character, its reason of being.
Here Elgar thought "in strings," as elsewhere
he "thinks in full score." The Serenade is a
favourite piece with amateur orchestras, and
one could wish that Elgar had written more
music of this type. He thinks well of the

Serenade ; even after the "Apostles," he said,
" I like it as well as anything I have done."   A
number of small pieces intervened between
this and his first published cantata, " The Black
Knight," Op. 25, produced by a Worcester
Choral Society in 1893, then heard at Wolver-
hampton and Birmingham, and before long all
over England. A setting of Longfellow's trans-
lation of Uhland's weird poem, " Der Schwarze
Ritter," the cantata is of the choral-ballad type,
the music modern with a touch of audacity,
the chorus only part of the means for obtaining
tone-colour, the orchestra treated with great
skill, the whole work dramatic, striking, pic-
turesque, and, above all, with a distinct individuality, an Elgar-flavour already detected by
the connoisseurs.   It is noteworthy that Elgar
calls " The Black Knight " a symphony for
chorus and orchestra.   The Choral Suite,
" From the Bavarian Highlands," is an instance
of the composer's versatility of mood ; here all
is facile and placid.   The spirit of his summer
holiday resort is caught, but the melodies are
his own. This Elgar is the Elgar of the Twelve
Voluntaries, the Coronation Ode, and the Pomp
and Circumstance Marches, of which, by the

way, the number is not two, but six. "Why
should a composer always write in an exacting
spirit?" he asks. "Why not relax the bow
occasionally? My conception of a composer's
duty includes his being a bard for the people.
He ought to write a popular tune sometimes.
The Coronation was a popular function. As to
the marches, I have been much among military
men, and I have wondered why the quick
march, which is what soldiers really march to,
has never been treated symphonically. Soldiers too often march to the most trivial music.
Why not try to give them something a little
better?" These words of Elgar may serve as
answer to certain hostile criticisms.

The Organ Sonata, Opus 28, was accepted
as strong and new, and "Lux Christi," later
named "The Light of Life," Op. 29, Elgar's
first choral work to be heard at a festival,
produced at the Worcester meeting of 1896,
confirmed the opinion of the few who saw in
the composer original creative power, with
adequate equipment of technique. The subject afforded scope for expressive writing
but public interest in the restoration of the
blind man's sight and the spiritual applica-

tion of the miracle lacked intensity, though the music is dramatic and the libretto, by the Rev. E. Capel-Cure, could hardly be bettered. Here are movements which in form, if not in spirit, remind us of the older choral writers, though the *leit-motiv* is used. The cantata did not become so popular as was predicted, but the introductory " Meditation," played everywhere, kept the name of Elgar in the programmes. A few weeks after the Worcester Festival came the North Staffordshire meeting at Hanley, and " King Olaf " was given to the world.

" King Olaf " was so much bigger than the " Lux Christi," that even those who best knew Elgar rubbed their eyes in something like amazement. It was stronger than the most sanguine had expected. The musicians who had believed that music had done its utmost were taken aback, and required a period of seclusion in order to grapple with the unexpected situation. By " King Olaf " many were convinced that there was still a possibility of something new; that striking individuality without extravagance was not altogether visionary; that the dry bones of science could still be clothed with life; that the old con-

D

trapuntists and the new impressionists had
not exhausted the permutations of artistic
melody and harmony; that, in short, an
original and powerful genius could fuse into
a consistent whole all that was best in the
old and new schools; could reconcile Bach
and Berlioz, Handel and Wagner, and all
this, not as a mere eclectic, but rather as
an innovator, an assimilator who had made
all his own; brilliant in invention, rich in
imagination, and a skilled craftsman in the
most subtle and recondite workmanship.

"King Olaf" is strong, graphic, giving a
sense of the folk-song, a savour of the sea,
an impression of the Berserker spirit. Elgar
has given invention free rein; is more himself
than ever; is breaking away from whatever
compound of influences had dominated before.
His orchestration is richer; he becomes auda-
cious. Effects heard later in "Gerontius" are
tried in "King Olaf"; a soprano air, doubled
in the bass two and three octaves below, is
weird in the one, awe-inspiring in the other.
"Olaf" displays a great variety of moods;
Longfellow's words are cleverly connected
and reinforced by Mr. H. A. Acworth. So

far Elgar has fared well with the librettists.
Fastidious as Mendelssohn, he is more fortu-
nate. Throughout "Olaf" is shown a greater
command of the theme-system, a magistral
handling to convince the most incredulous.
Only in the solo writing is there room for
doubt as to whether the master has attained
his full stature. From the Saga Theme at
the beginning to the Death of Olaf and the
Epilogue, all is consistent, homogeneous, fas-
cinating. Not a dull number, not a needless
bar. The Challenge of Thor, the Return of
Olaf, the Conversion, the Episodes of Gudrun,
the Wraith of Odin, and Sigrid and Thyri,
succeed each other naturally, interest growing
to the end. Here in the realms of imagination
we feel the very breath of romance; we are
in touch with the noblest old-world chivalry.
And after this the same mind produces the
"Cockaigne" overture and "The Apostles"
oratorio. A genius of many facets, which may
be its secret. A receptive nature, saturated
with the tints that make the rainbow of
beauty.

After "King Olaf" the next works that arrest
attention are the "Te Deum" and "Benedic-

tus," written for the Hereford Festival of 1897;
Elgar, the Roman Catholic, choosing the
English words, while Sir Hubert Parry for a
later Hereford Festival, and Sir Charles Stan-
ford for a Leeds Festival, elected for the Latin.
There is no setting of the Ambrosian hymn
that can be compared with Elgar's in point of
distinctive character. It may be argued that
the music is not church music, that it is not
English music, that it is not good music. To
all or any of these charges one might listen
with patience and due show of respect. Further, one might believe that between Purcell's
"Te Deum" and that of Elgar there were
better "Te Deums" than Elgar's, and that
Dvorak's or Verdi's outdid him in freedom of
style. But it could never be maintained that
there was a "Te Deum" of like mood and
feeling. The introduction is calculated to
startle good men and true whose standard is
found in the work of English church musicians. The very phrasing of the words is new
and alarming. There is, however, much deli-
cious music, full enjoyment of which comes to
many only after a struggle with prepossessions.
The short strain for orchestra before the words,

" Make them to be numbered with Thy Saints,"
may be specially commended to Elgar students
as Elgar-in-excelsis. It recurs, in triple measure,
before " Vouchsafe, O Lord," and is given to
the voices at " O Lord, in Thee have I trusted."
This and the passage at the mezzoforte of the
introduction are so Elgaresque that they sound
like soul-transcriptions. In them we have the
quintessence of the dominant Elgar mood.

The "Caractacus" cantata, though magnifi-
cent, and, moreover, eminently successful on
production, did not take hold of the British
imagination. Not far from Elgar's house, the
great hill known as the Herefordshire Beacon,
with its vast system of pre-historic fortifications
attributed to the Silures, rears its scarred
flanks to the clouds, and this, no doubt, inspired Elgar with the "Caractacus" idea. The
cantata is built on modern lines, and in point
of structure may be compared with "King
Olaf," and though perhaps with more elaboration, possibly with an occasional want of
theme-dignity, rare fault in this composer.
Still there is marked advance : the solo voices
are treated with greater consideration. There
is marked progress of orchestral technique.

"Caractacus" did not touch the masses, was not played upon the barrel-organs, but it served the great purpose of marking the composer's increasing recognition. For some occult reason the Leeds and Birmingham Festivals are accounted superior in prestige to the Three Choir Festivals. To be heard at Leeds is to be received among those born in the purple. Received, for the moment only. It is for the man to make good his footing, to sustain his claim, or for ever; after to hold his peace. The Festivals of Leeds and Birmingham give prestige to success. But failure at either is irreparable. To go down at a Three Choir Festival is not so serious—there is consolation in the company of the majority. You are only one of the noble army of martyrs. To fail at the bigger festivals is to fall like Lucifer, never to rise again.

Elgar did not fall. His star was in the ascendant. Step by step he moved from one coign of vantage to another, rising always. "Caractacus" is numbered Op. 35. The "Enigma" orchestral piece is Op. 36. What the solution of the " Enigma " may be, nobody but the composer knows. The theme is a counterpoint on some well-known melody which is never heard, the variations are the theme seen through the personalities of friends, with an intermezzo and a coda, the last added at the request of friends aided and abetted by Dr. Richter, who accepted the work on its merits, having received the score in Vienna from his agent in London, and who at the time had not met with the composer. The extraordinary ingenuity of Elgar in varying the rather unpromising theme is as surprising as his intimate knowledge of the orchestra, that vast repository of mysteries. The "Enigma" variations, "toured" by Richter's band, set the seal on Elgar's reputation. Richter did for Elgar what he had done for Wagner thirty years before. England was won for Wagner by Richter and the "Tannhauser" Overture. England was won for Elgar by Richter and the "Enigma" variations. The noble song-cycle of "Sea Pictures" for contralto, produced in the same year, showed Elgar's versatility once more ; and then came "Gerontius," which was to make his reputation international, and to demonstrate that, with opportunity and encouragement, the really strong man goes from strength to strength.

It was "King Olaf" that raised Elgar to master-rank, and the "Enigma" variations that made him widely known. But for historical importance, neither of these works can compete with his cantata "The Dream of Gerontius," produced at the Birmingham Triennial Festival of 1900, a memorable epoch in the annals of English music. The success of "Caractacus" at Leeds led the Birmingham authorities to the consideration of Elgar's merit, discovery of which had unaccountably escaped them for several years. And so it came to pass that "Gerontius" was completed, not written for the Festival. The music of "Gerontius" was no extemporaneous production. From the year 1889 Elgar had been studying the poem, a copy of which was given to him as a wedding present by Father Knight, of Worcester. Not an ordinary copy, but one in which Gordon's favourite passages were indicated throughout. The cantata existed in Elgar's mind when the commission came. For years he had been making sketches, at all times and places, just as the ideas came ; selecting, rejecting, jotting down items when out walking ; making memoranda on the return home, the whole gradually ripening in his mind, slowly assuming shape, condensing from the possible to the actual, like the nebulous haze of which new worlds are made. Other irons were in the fire. Elgar confesses to being engaged on twenty works at once. But "Gerontius" went on intermittently, maturing, growing as the oak grows, slowly perhaps, but naturally and enduringly. There was no hurry : nobody requested an epoch-making work ; nobody expected an epoch-making work from Elgar. That is, nobody among the Festival authorities. It may be that the circumstances suited the composer whose failing leans to over-fastidiousness, and who, above all things, desires to satisfy himself, his severest critic. Not that he is essentially slow. So far he has not, like Mozart, dashed off three symphonies in six weeks ; but his facility is remarkable, and in the matter of scoring, one or two accomplished feats rank with the phenomenal. A musician who can throw off thirty sheets of heaviest scoring in a week need not be ashamed to meet his enemies in the gate.

Edward Elgar was not the first to ponder a musical setting of "Gerontius." The subject was tempting. From the earliest period of which we have any record, the mind of man has striven to peer beyond the portals of the grave. And whether it was Plato arguing for immortality, or Shakespeare discussing the Undiscovered Country, "the bourne from which no traveller returns," the speculation has ever been, as it ever must be, of highest interest to the minds of men. Of all attempts to remove the veil, perhaps that of Cardinal Newman is the most powerful, the most absorbing. The death-bed of a dear friend inspired the poem, which was first printed in the midsummer of 1865, some thirty years before any composer, greatly daring, ventured to set it to music. And no wonder. The theme is a lofty one, and proportionately exacting. Gerontius on his death-bed dreams that his soul speeds through space to the invisible realm where the ministering angels of the great white throne wait with ineffable welcome. The way has terrors; there is doubt, there is apprehension. The mocking cries of demons are heard, fiendish discords clash with

the celestial strains of angels and archangels
and all the company of heaven. From first to
last the poet deals with themes which are at
once entrancing to minds of religious inclina-
tion, and eminently susceptible of musical
illustration. Here was a glorious opportunity,
a wonderful libretto that in an age which was
thought to have utilised every opportunity for
oratorio, was lying like a derelict avoided by
mariners as being too heavy with treasure.
The poet is mystic, rapt, sublime, as far re-
moved from the prosaic materialism of the age
as Thomas of Celano, reputed writer of the
" Dies Iræ." To wed the lofty phantasy of
Newman to adequate music required a like
aloofness of spirit as well as equal inspiration.
After a whole generation of waiting, the hour
came, and with it the man.

The work of Edward Elgar has been accepted as adequate by judges of independent
thought. The English public did not at
first find in " Gerontius " an art-work of
authentic inspiration. They listened with becoming respect, but they were disappointed.
Elgar spoke a language of which they knew
not the idiom. They looked for the suave airs

and overwhelming choruses of orthodox oratorio. Their conceptions were conventional.
Consciously or unconsciously every sacred
work of any pretension is compared with
"Messiah" and "Elijah," which were long
regarded as the nearest approach to the unat-
tainable ideal. The rank and file of the first
hearers of "Gerontius" expected melodic
parallels to "He shall feed His flock" and "O
rest in the Lord," with brave choral outbursts
like the "Hallelujah Chorus" and "Thanks
be to God." And so it was, that, under the
influence of conservative preposessions, they
felt at the close as though they had been sent
empty away. Even the musicians were doubt-
ful. The thing was so strange, so unprece-
dented, and, from the accustomed view-point,
so revolutionary, that all except the most advanced took time to consider. The conservative mind is necessarily slow. There was a
period of neglect which promised to be indefi-
nite, and possibly to stretch out until the crack
of doom. Then came the Düsseldorf performances and the outspoken verdict of the main body
of German critics, whose prevailing tone was enthusiastic welcome mingled with astonishment.

The story of Elgar's appreciation in Germany constitutes a remarkable phase of a remarkable career, and deserves a whole volume to itself.   Long ago Schumann said : " English composer, no composer ; " and the saying sank deep into the hearts of his countrymen, who in later years looked upon English music as meaning Arthur Sullivan and the " Mikado." England was admired for her energy, her success in colonisation, her enormous commercial prosperity ; and the best German thinkers held that herein lay her strength.   And for this reason they declared that her art-feeling was atrophied, and that she was destitute of the spirit that could produce a Beethoven, or even a Mendelssohn.   No serious English music was heard at any great German festival.   No English composer had been honoured at the Lower Rhine meetings since the days of Onslow, seventy years before " Gerontius " ; and Onslow, who could hardly be called an Englishman at all, remains uncertain.   The musical intellect of Germany had long regarded the regular festival-commissioned examples of English oratorio as more or less feeble echoes of Handel and Mendelssohn, without distinctive character, puny weaklings of German paternity, born in a land where serious music was an exotic insusceptible of acclimatisation. From time to time strong appeals against what was called the injustice of this estimate, which had become traditional, were made without avail. Germany obstinately refused to listen. German programmes remained without English works of importance, and German musicians were stigmatised by their English *confrères* as jealous and intolerant. Under these circumstances, which were notorious, the bare fact of the inclusion of Elgar's work in the programme of the Düsseldorf meeting had a significance which appealed irresistibly to Elgar's countrymen, the verdict of the German press aroused renewed attention, and " Gerontius," which had suffered severely from a bad performance on its production at Birmingham, was reconsidered. Soon it was heard in most of the musical centres of Great Britain, and everywhere with approbation. Little by little conductors and their forces, and, in due course, their audiences, grasped the idea that the work was to be judged by its intrinsic merit, and not by comparison with standards more or less

outworn ; that while the older masters looked
upon form as a primary essential, Elgar
attached a supreme importance to expression,
and that much might be said for the logical
accuracy of the later view.

The subject of "Gerontius," we can well
believe, peculiarly appealed to Elgar's temperament. From the first we have a mystic
atmosphere. The opening strain of the prelude indicates a sense of apprehension at
thought of the Unknown. A short link, expressive of fear, introduces a prayer which
again leads to a movement representing
the troubled slumber of sickness, and this
again to the sorrow theme, one of the most
poignant and strikingly original in the whole
work. After this the prayer theme is repeated
fortissimo, and a gradual diminuendo on a
reference to the sorrow theme, introduces the
"Go forth" theme, which, with others given
in the epitomistic introduction, is later heard
from the voices, either in solo or chorus.
The slumber theme and the theme which expresses dread of the Unknown are repeated,
and with what has been called the death theme
this profoundly impressive movement ends.

To proceed in detail through the cantata is
neither practicable nor desirable. The structure of the prelude, roughly hinted above, will
convey to those familiar with the modern
method of working with leading motives some
notion of the main framework of "Gerontius."
The themes already indicated are heard again
and again, singly or in combination ; sometimes given with elementary simplicity, sometimes with an extreme subtilty that demands
from the hearer closest attention and keenest
critical faculty. One recognises why the music
failed to succeed at once. The average concert-
goer was not prepared either for the strangeness of the mood or the complexity of the
music, a strangeness which startled, a complexity which demanded unwonted mental
exertion. In Britain the popular notion of
music is of something pleasant and ear-tick-
ling ; something lightly sensuous, as well as
gently stimulating and refreshing. English
audiences are seldom inclined to the studious,
and therefore are rarely prepared to take
serious composition with deep seriousness.
Their conception of the loftiest music is, in
the main, sentimental and though senti-

mentality may be secular or religious, it
remains but sentimentality with hardly a
chemical trace of the intellectual. Not that
the English are alone in this weakness. It is
this false conception which has given the
fatuous name of "The Moonlight" to one of
the most tragic sonatas of Beethoven, to cite a
solitary instance of its shallow self-betrayal.
No wonder that "Gerontius" fell flat. That
the work had a certain beauty could not be
denied : here and there the forceful sincerity
of the composer carried momentary conviction. There were passages that ran in the
head, not as snatches of tune that could be
hummed, but as impressions that remained in
the brain though they could not be hummed.
Or perhaps it would be better to say
that the impression was in the heart. Despite a certain doubtfulness, the music had
you in its grip and would not let you go.
Repeated hearings deepened the impression
of power, and slowly conviction grew that
here was a work of extreme subjectiveness, of
wonderful individuality, conjoined with adequate equipment of technique and vivifying
creative genius. Surely the sincerity of Elgar

in " Gerontius " can scarcely be matched in
the whole realm of music. The successive
pages range over a vast field of emotions, from
the very Alpha to the Omega of religious
sensibility. Hideous demoniac outcries have
their antitheses in hymns of celestial thanks-
giving, and between these extremes we have
the self-communings of Gerontius, the re-
assuring utterances of the Guardian Angel and
the Angel of the Agony, the music everywhere
conveying a sense of deep passion, masterly
command of means, and, best of all, the
absolute sincerity without which no art can
be truly great. The subject of " Gerontius "
recalls Strauss and the "Tod und Verklärung ; "
but here, at all events, the two masters have
little in common. Strauss impresses me as
looking from the outside, as taking his inspiration from external things. With Elgar
the opposite impression is paramount. Moreover, the English composer appeals to me,
for one, as more purely intellectual, more deli-
cately refined, as well as more spiritually
emotional. Many, indeed, find in Elgar a
preponderance of the emotional over the
intellectual. This is no doubt a question of

the personal equation.   Every hearer is under
the dominion of the heredity, education and
environment which are summed in his temperament.   Many   musicians,   especially   those
engaged in the service of the Church, are in-
sensibly biassed by their diatonic proclivities,
by the Puritan plainness which in some
quarters is thought to be the only music well-
pleasing to the Lord.   No doubt Elgar in
"Gerontius" is influenced by the higher
colour affected in the Roman Church, in
whose music he took active part during his
childhood, youth, and much of his manhood.
No doubt it is true that the emotional side of
"Gerontius" is unwontedly rich, but no
cultured and faithful musician can hear the
music or that of "Olaf" or of "The Apostles"
without conviction of an intellectuality at
once all-pervading and intense.   Moreover, the
educated listener will in successive hearings
discover, slowly perhaps but surely, an extraordinary subtlety of intellectual comment on
the librettos.   It may be submitted that these
are factors that make for immortality.   First I
discover in Elgar a very audacity of sincerity,
without a moment's fear for the result; an

immovable determination to follow truth, as
he sees it, wherever it may lead, and to whatever fate may impend. With Elgar there is
no temporising. You may follow him to the
heights, or you may choose to linger below;
that is your own affair. Then, given the
ardent artistic temperament, enthusiasm, invention and a purely musical nature hardly
surpassed among the moderns, and in addition
an easy command of every modern resource,
whether of theory or practice, and we have
indeed the equipment of an artistic conqueror.

Throughout "Gerontius" is seen the further
advancement of the musical development of
the last hundred years in the direction of expression. In this respect it has been claimed
that Elgar is the greatest musician since
Beethoven, possibly the greatest since Bach.
Without instituting the smallest comparison
where comparison would be profitless, it may
be suggested that Elgar would never, could
never, set sacred words in the modern binary
form, after the manner of Haydn in "Insanæ
et vanæ curiæ" or Mozart in "Splendente te
Deus." With all his modernity Elgar's method

is rather a reversion to Bach, whose Saint
Matthew Passion has been the model of
expressiveness through the whole of the
modern period. Elgar in "Gerontius" ex-
hibits greater power in the expressive and
emotional domain than any other modern
writer, not excepting Brahms in his Requiem.
Moreover, his strength is not always shown in
miracles of ipolyphony. It has been said of
Mozart that he obtained great effects by simple
means. And despite the common reproach
that Elgar relies on elaboration and extraordinary combinations, it can be shown that
his greatest work is often easiest to grasp.
Even the unæsthetic are strangely moved by
the Litany which follows the chorus " Rescue
him " in "Gerontius." What is the magic of
that simple strain ? There can be but one
answer. The succession of chords, seen in
print, looks simple enough. But when heard,
imagination is carried back to the middle ages,
to " cathedrals dim and vast, where the majestic
organ rolled Contrition from its mouths of
gold." No work of Elgar is wanting in similar
instances of singular power with simple means.
In " King Olaf " the chorus, " Like torrents in

summer," exemplifies this faculty, the very
hall-mark of golden genius. Passing to later
work, who can fail to be struck with the
wondrous force of such passages as the setting
in "The Apostles" of the words, "To give
unto them that mourn a garland for ashes"
with their continuation ? Again may be cited
the words of Jesus at the wayside, a recitative following an introduction that seems an
echo of the flight of Gerontius to heaven,
"Blessed are the poor in spirit." Another
example worthy of study is the chorus, "Draw
out thy soul to the hungry," though study will
hardly reveal its secret. There is, too, something of the arch-mage in a later chorus.
"Blessed are they which have been sorrowful,"
which, like all the passages quoted, has the
remarkable quality of producing the deepest
emotional stirrings in those who hear it most
often—a suggestive fact. The story of the
overwhelming effect of Beethoven's Fifth
symphony on Lesueur, the master of Berlioz,
is not without its counterpart relating to the
music of Elgar. A chorus-master of first rank
and of such vast experience and constant
practice that one might be pardoned the

assumption that his musical emotions were
calloused by long usage, assures me that the
short passage, "Proclaim unto them that dwell
on the earth," which occupies about a page
and a half of "The Apostles," produces on him
an effect which can only be described as almost
paralysing.   Minds in affinity with the mystic
mood are similarly affected by certain passages
in "Gerontius," and it has been observed that
few are agreed as to the point at which the
highest plane is reached, and further that each
successive hearing is apt to induce change of
opinion, facts not without a subtle suggestive-
ness of their own.

In "Gerontius" Elgar has displayed daring
subjectiveness, vivid imagination and perfect
equipment.   Yet without beauty all these
were as nothing.   And there is beauty in pro-
fusion.   To follow the sounds with the words
is to experience the highest enjoyment.   As
absolute   music   the   introduction   and   the
choruses are beautiful exceedingly.   Elgar's
mastery of polyphony is never pedantic ; there
is always a reason, a special meaning.   "When
I write fewer than the usual four vocal parts,"
says Elgar, "it is because I do not want four.

When I write fourteen, it is because I want them all." "Gerontius" has examples of fourteen parts, yet everywhere the psychic impression is so strong that the most scholastic hearer is apt to be unconscious of the technique because his faculties are absorbed in the sublime.

VII

"THE APOSTLES"

As we have seen, the germ of "The Apostles" oratorio dates from Elgar's school-days, some twenty years before his first acquaintance with Newman's poem of "Gerontius." Wherefore the idea of his having, on the spur of the moment, written it for the Birmingham Festival of 1903, must be dismissed as fallacious. A few days before its production he said: "There is a popular error concerning musical commissions for festivals. Some people seem to think that a composer sits waiting, like the false witnesses of Westminster Hall, men who, in the olden time, stood about with straws in their shoes, ready to swear anything to order. It is a mistake to suppose that a musician stands waiting to be hired, like a man in a fair. A composer worthy the name never waits for an order before setting to work. He

is always thinking out works, always making
sketches. He may complete a work for a
festival. Another favourite delusion is this :
that a composer cannot do his best, his most
inspired work, under such a commission to
complete. The contrary is the case. When
he knows that his music will be produced in
the most perfect manner, with the best prin-
cipals, the best band, the best chorus possible,
and with every accessory he may demand, the
natural result is that he rises to the occasion.
He is encouraged, inspired, and generally
stimulated. ‘ The Apostles ’ oratorio was
projected before ‘ Gerontius.’ I have been
thinking it out since boyhood, and have been
selecting the words for years, many years. I
am my own librettist. Some day I will give
you my ideas on the relationship between
librettist and composer.”

That Elgar is a daring librettist must be
conceded. The character of Judas is set forth
on the plane of the higher criticism. Elgar
takes the old view now accounted modern,
that Judas had no intention of delivering
Christ to death, but rather that he desired to
afford opportunities for the display of a God-

like power which must have compelled the
Jews to acclaim Him as their King. The sin
of Judas was an attempt to know better than
the Master ; whence came awful consequences.
Again, a certain utterance concerning Mary
Magdalene is given to a chorus of women.
"A man said it," the composer remarked,
"a man said it in those ancient days. But
it is women who say such things to-
day."

"What is my method of writing? When I
propose such a work as this I first of all read
everything I can lay my hands on which bears
on the subject directly or indirectly, meditating
on all that I have sifted out as likely to serve
my purpose, and blending it with my musical
conceptions. Every personality appears to
me in a musical dress. I suppose that all
who read novels form mental pictures of the
characters. So with me : I involuntarily give
to each a musical character, clothe each with
a musical expression, in this case Judas, Peter,
and the rest. I do not seek for character-
motives : they come, in all places, at all
seasons. I never sit down and say, 'Now I
will compose.' The thing is inconceivable to

me. What comes, comes of itself ; of course
I am often thinking in music."

If the first performance of "Gerontius" gave
rise to doubt, the production of "The Apostles"
gave rise to tenfold more doubt. The difficulty with Elgar is that he will not rest and be
thankful. The critics find it hard to keep pace
with him. Swinging up the slopes of Parnassus
with ever-increasing length of stride, he leaves
them panting, breathless, declaring that the
ascent is too steep, or, if less candid, that the
last peak was the highest, and that further
climbing is but climbing down. And once
again the general attitude may be recognised
as inevitable. Mr. A. J. Balfour has told us that
though "the public often want some new thing,
they do not often want a new kind of thing.
And accordingly it commonly, though not
invariably, happens, that when the new thing
appears, it is welcomed at first by the few, and
only gradually, by the force of fashion and
otherwise, conquers the genuine admiration of
the many. The true artist is moved in no
small measure by the desire that his work shall
be his own; no pale reflection of another's
methods, but an expression of himself in his

own language." This passage, written long before our composer was famous, might have related directly to Elgar and "The Apostles."

The later work was harder to write than "Gerontius," and is harder to understand. In the earlier composition Elgar had the advantage of a unified libretto with a single central idea, clearly and strongly stated and universally interesting. Moreover, the subject was one of mystic idealism, in dealing with which the composer was accorded utmost licence. Since all was beyond our ken, he might imagine as he would. True, there was doubt; but time and the German pæans worked wonders, and "Gerontius" was accepted as a masterpiece. Then we tacitly told Elgar to pause awhile; to let well alone; to be content with the eminence already reached, and not to strain onward and upward in obedience to an imaginary "Excelsior"; imaginary, because inaudible to us. True to his star, Elgar kept on the rising track after the manner of his like in every age. The true genius is a Finder, a Leader. He lives in the age to come, is often so far in advance as to be almost out of sight, a mere dot on the horizon. The critic is

dominated by the memory of past ideals. He
has no *locus standi* to deliver judgment on the
real pioneers of art. We have only to remember what was said of Mozart, of Beethoven,
of Schumann, of Wagner. With the past
before us we may note some carpings at Elgar
and " The Apostles." It is said that he is too
chromatic ; the same was said of Mozart ;
that he is weak in counterpoint ; Hande is
charged with saying this of Gluck ; John
Hullah certainly said it of Beethoven. More
especially is it alleged that the work lacks
coherence and consistency of style. The origin
of this last charge will be seen from a brief
description of the libretto plan.

Elgar has chosen the words from the widest
range of Scripture, apocryphal and other.
The work is divided into two parts, which are
again subdivided into seven, which form a
natural sequence thus : 1. The Calling of the
Apostles ; 2. By the Wayside ; 3. By the Lake
of Galilee ; 4. The Betrayal ; 5. Golgotha ; 6.
At the Sepulchre ; 7. The Ascension. The
seven divisions are again divided into scenes
from which arises a certain complexity de-
manding patient study and a certain pious

enthusiasm, following on a certain degree of
artistic faith. The oratorio requires time to
grow upon the listener, who needs the successive hearings that at once familiarise and
illumine. There is at first but a dim view of
the matter; we lose our bearings; fail to
follow the abounding subtleties of allusion.
The thing is deep, and the age is not given
to profundity. We see in part; as through a
glass, darkly. We recognise beauty and
colossal command of resource, for a parallel to
which we must revert to Bach and Wagner.
What we at first fail to realise is the essential
coherency. But if the thing as a whole comes
slowly, it comes. After many days the mental
Shofar sounds, and "it shines." Then only is
the rich treasure appreciated, the poetry and
greatness of conception and execution esti-
mated at their real worth.

For one, I have no doubt that in the end
Elgar's first instalment of his projected trilogy
of "The Apostles" will be esteemed an advance on "Gerontius," not only in point of
technique but also in loftiness of conception,
in general nobility of thought, and even in
originality of invention. If "Gerontius" had

the defects of its qualities, these would be an emotionalism tending to effeminacy and a want of reticence where reticence would be the higher art. It is admissible to suggest that the score of "Gerontius" is over-elaborated, and to refer the composer to the example of Beethoven, who laboured to clear his symphonies of the redundant. The charge of over-elaboration may be made against "The Apostles," the other charges must fail. The later work is of more masculine fibre, and, with all its passion, has greater reserve. And greater reserve means greater dignity. There is the same religious fervour, something of the same awe and mystery, with higher nobility and deeper strength. There is also the same Elgar mood, one of the chief characteristics of which is the ineffable tenderness which to some minds savours of feminism, to others merely of the impassioned character of the Romanist ritual (as contrasted with the Puritan), under whose influence the composer spent his most impressionable years. The Elgar atmosphere is unique. Here he borrows from none. No doubt Elgar is deeply indebted to his predecessors. "The greatest genius is the most

indebted man." In one or other of his works,
we are reminded of Wagner, of Berlioz, of
Tchaikovsky, just as in the works of these composers we are reminded of others. But the
mood is different: the hypnotic effect is
different: the Elgar impression is of Elgar
alone. To listen to "Gerontius" or "The
Apostles" is to be left in an emotional state
wholly unlike that induced by any other composer. If there is a trace of Wagner, it is a
Wagner of more tenderness; if of Berlioz, a
Berlioz of greater depth and reality; if of
Tchaikovsky, a Tchaikovsky of sweet reason-
ableness and celestial hope. From end to end
"The Apostles" is permeated with the most
subtle essence of the composer's thought and
feeling. It is this quintessence of sincerity that
gives power. Herein is the secret, the grand
arcanum. It is the very unveiling of the soul.
It was said of Beethoven's Ninth Symphony
that therein was the tone-poet's spirit expressed
in harmonies. Something of the kind might
be written on the scores of "The Apostles"
and "Gerontius."

It is admitted that to hear "The Apostles"
once, and once only, is to be dissatisfied. The

F

first impression is that of a beautiful panorama
of which the various scenes are not satisfac-
torily connected. There seems a want of co-
hesiveness, and, looking to the libretto, gathered
from a wide area, you are inclined to suggest
that the work lacks the concentration and unity
for which the composer was indebted to the
poem of "Gerontius." The beauty of the
music is undeniable. The power of representing varied emotions is equally beyond argu-
ment. Originality of theme-conception and
amazing technique of warp and woof command
the admiration of the musician. The note of
cloistral meditation, peculiar to Elgar, pervades
the whole with an unearthly beauty. And yet
even the faithful hover between doubt and
admiration. They speak of sketchiness, of non-
homogeneity, of rich promise and but partial
performance; of noble texts without adequate
sermons. The more self-confident talk of
Elgar's limitations, forgetting that the critic
may have limitations too.

The trouble lies not in any defect of the
composer, but in the stupendous complexity of
the music, which only reveals itself after much
artistic fasting and prayer. After one hearing

we stand, as it were, too near. To hear the
oratorio gradually at rehearsals, with time to
study the connections, the relationships, the
points of contact between the various scenes,
is to experience a real revelation. Even then
a first performance usually falls short of expec-
tation; for while it is possible to recognise
splendid choruses, powerful characterisation,
and a host of beauties of almost every con-
ceivable kind, the sum of the whole leaves a
certain hesitancy of decision. Further study
of the score, more rehearsals and a second
performance clear this away. It is as though
one had stood too close to a great cathedral
window with seven lights, each with several
pictured divisions, every one with manifest
beauty of its own, but only part of the whole.
And then it is as though one had receded,
keeping the whole in gaze and noting that with
larger view came gradual fusion into glorious
unity.

With reference to this crucial question of
unity it may be submitted that Elgar has
achieved the unity proposed. His libretto is
built on the lines of Greek tragedy. The Greek
tragedians did not trouble with explanatory

detail. The people knew the stories, and the poet's aim was but the heightening of leading incidents by action and environment. So with Elgar in " The Apostles." He assumes that people know the story with which he deals, and, setting forth its main features, he leaves something to the educated imagination. In assuming that musical critics are acquainted with the New Testament, Elgar may have erred, but it is only fair to state the principle on which he has worked. Further, his thought on unity, using the term in its all-embracing sense, may well be given in this connection. Elgar holds strongly to the art-necessity of consistency. He once said, " I am a follower of Sir Charles Eastlake, who in one of his art-lectures says that ' consistency of convention ' is essential in pictorial art. So in music. My interest in this is so great that I could talk on the theme for hours." To illustrate a part of his meaning he took the score of " Don Giovanni" to the piano and played portions of several numbers. "No matter what the mood," he continued, "in the lighter scenes or the most tragic, all is on the same level. There is the same creative force, the same degree of inspiration. Every

extended work must be coherent and consistent
from beginning to end. If you adopt this for-
mula of the deeper consistency, you will discover why certain things jar on you, if in an
artistic frame of mind. Apply it to oratorio.
You may perhaps remember instances in which
the magnetic feeling is cut off in order to give
the chorus a chance, when at the moment a
chorus is not a consistent development."

. As to complaints of want of beauty—and such
complaints have been heard—it avails little to
speak. *De gustibus non disputandum est.*
Difference in taste implies difference in the
very fibre of our being. Those who differ
widely stand on different planes of development. Between them is a space which only
time and culture can bridge. What of the
different standards of beauty that have from
time to time been set up by mankind? What
of the different standards upheld by different
races? Why do some prefer the tom-tom to
the Ninth Symphony? When we remember
the music that seemed beautiful to us long
years ago, and contrast it with what now seems
beautiful, we are tempted to declare that the
sense of beauty is mirage, illusion. It has

been said that beauty in music is in the heart and brain of the hearer. Which is a summing up of the common consciousness so often in line with the profoundest philosophy. So much for the plaint of such as find no beauty or not enough in " The Apostles," which has also been called dull and monotonous. To which it may be replied that if we make entertainment our standard, we must condemn Dante and Michael Angelo and Titian's " Last Supper," and Rubens' " Descent from the Cross," with a host of art-works of the more serious kind. Those who seek entertainment in oratorio are certainly in the majority; applause proved that long ago. The weakest numbers are always most popular, as being nearest the intellect of the average hearer. To this majority the pervasive tenderness and solemn mystic beauty of " The Apostles " can never strongly appeal.

The technical difficulty of Elgar's choral works has been insisted upon by the echoes whose critical stock-in-trade consists of safe catchwords. Elgar is not often technically difficult for voices. That there are dangerous passages is true enough, but they are not dangerous by reason of the composer's want of contrapuntal considerateness. Rather is it by reason of momentary want of support to the voices, or to a succession of harmonies which incur risk of false intonation. Practised chorus-masters find him far less difficult than Brahms. It was at first the fashion to speak of Elgar as essentially an orchestral writer, as a one-sided man who knew nothing of voices On the contrary, Elgar as a vocal writer is at least on a level with the best composers living, if not altogether supreme, which last bold proposition has been urged by some. Not that he constructs greater vocal effects than one or two others, but that while his great climaxes rank with the finest in existence, he has originated vocal combinations of great power and beauty in short phrases, examples of which have already been cited. As an orchestral expert, Elgar has no rival except Strauss, and in knowledge of the poetry of the individual instruments Elgar is probably first. Replying to a query as to his creation of new orchestral combinations, he once said, " They say so, but I never in my life said to myself, 'This shall be new; I will do something novel.'

The fact is I mentally hear the instruments, and when scoring put down what I feel that the sentiment of the words, if there be words, demands for the most perfect expression attainable. So far as I am concerned the thing is already complete in my mind : to make others feel it as I do is the trouble. If I could only write as fast as I think !"

The Elgar Festival, unique honour to a unique personality, displayed the amazing variety and extraordinary scope of Elgar's genius. No test could be more severe. Apply it to the great names in music, and we find that only the greatest could emerge with equal honour, with equal triumph. From which it may be argued that we may anticipate the verdict of posterity as to the final position of Edward Elgar's niche in the Temple of Fame. What Wagner did for opera, from the point at which it was left by Mozart and Weber, Elgar is doing for oratorio from the point at which it was left by Handel and Mendelssohn, and, as many believe, with equal inspiration. This is but a part of his work, but were this his solitary achievement he would have richly earned a conspicuous place among the immortals.

EDWARD ELGAR'S WORKS

EDWARD ELGAR'S WORKS

21. Minuet : small orchestra.
22. Six easy exercises : violin with pianoforte accompaniment.
23. Spanish Serenade : chorus and orchestra.
24. Etudes Caractéristiques : violin.
25. The Black Knight : cantata for chorus and orchestra (called by the composer a symphony for chorus and orchestra).
26. Part songs, S.S.C., with two violins obbligato.
27. From the Bavarian Highlands : choral suite for chorus and orchestra.
28. Sonata : organ.
29. Lux Christi : oratorio.
30. King Olaf : cantata.
31. Two songs.
32. Imperial march : orchestra.
33. The Banner of Saint George : cantata.
34. Te Deum and Benedictus : chorus and orchestra.
35. Caractacus : cantata.
36. Enigma variations on an original theme : orchestra.
37. Sea Pictures : song-cycle for contralto, with orchestral accompaniment.
38. The Dream of Gerontius.
39. Pomp and Circumstance : military marches for orchestra.
40. Cockaigne : concert overture.
41. Two songs.
42. Grania and Diarmid : incidental music.
43. Dream Children : two sketches for small orchestra.
44. Coronation Ode : cantata.
45. Part Songs, T.T.B.B. : from the Greek anthology.
46. MS.
47. MS.

48. MS.

49. The Apostles : oratorio.

50. In the South : concert overture.

Of the unpublished works with opus number the early ones are: Quintet for Wind, String Quartet, and Sonata for pianoforte and violin.

The later ones are: Falstaff, concert overture; a String Quartet; and the unnamed pendant to Cockaigne, showing the reverse of the joyous picture therein drawn.

Several short works have been published without opus number, and a large number exist in manuscript in addition to the list given above, which has the approval of Dr. Elgar.

HENRY J. WOOD

By ROSA NEWMARCH

Vol. I.—"LIVING MASTERS OF MUSIC." Illustrated

Morning Post.—"Apart from its biographical interest the volume is remarkable on account of the author's knowledge and critical acumen, as well as the excellence of its literary style."

Daily Telegraph.—"The writer need offer no apology, either for the task she has undertaken or for her manner of discharging it."

Daily News.—"She has so tempered her appreciation that, while the Queen's Hall conductor is placed on a high pedestal, the most captious of critics must admit that the estimate of his powers is just. The biographical portion of the book is full of information. . . . The student of modern music and the intelligent amateur should possess Mrs. Newmarch's book."

Academy.—"The new series makes a promising start. . . . Mrs. Newmarch analyses in a very discriminating manner the characteristics of Mr. Wood's artistic methods, and has produced a very interesting volume."

Literary World.—"To all who care for music and the development of musical taste in England this brief, pleasantly-written, and informing little book will be welcome."

Westminster Gazette.—"Precisely what he has accomplished in the course of those ten years is set forth with admirable judgment and discrimination in these well-written pages."

Pall Mall Gazette.—"Mrs. Newmarch's writing always has a very readable quality."

St. James's Gazette.—"She has found both a remarkably interesting subject and one which will immediately appeal to every music-lover. . . . Mrs. Newmarch has shown in a remarkable degree those qualities of tact and impartiality of which, in her preface, she modestly disavows the possession."

Musical Opinion.—"Mrs. Newmarch's interesting little monograph . . . makes an excellent beginning for a very promising series—a series for which we hope our readers will find a place on their shelves."

Musical News.—"Mrs. Newmarch has shown perfect tact and an excellent temper. . . . She must now be classed as a practised and brilliant writer. . . . The present volume is the most important and successful of all her prose writings."

Musical Herald.—"All who listen to the Queen's Hall Orchestra should get this book, so as to understand something of the soul which animates its performances."

Music.—"Charmingly written. . . . Mr. Wood is one of the greatest executive musicians England has produced. . . . The book should be read by all his admirers and detractors."

JOHN LANE, PUBLISHER, LONDON AND NEW YORK

MUSICAL ANNOUNCEMENTS

BECHSTEIN.
BREITKOPF & HÄRTEL.
S. P. ERARD.
METZLER & CO.
JOHN BROADWOOD & SONS, LTD.
MISS ROBINSON.
ORCHESTRELLE CO.
JOSEPH WILLIAMS, LTD.
SCHOTT & CO.
DALHOUSIE YOUNG'S MUSIC TO "SIX
    FAIRY PLAYS."
"LIVING MASTERS OF MUSIC."
"OLD ENGLISH SONGS AND DANCES."
ARCHIBALD RAMSDEN, LTD.

❧❧ BECHSTEIN HALL ❧❧
WIGMORE STREET, LONDON, W.

METZLER PIANO PLAYER

(WITH PATENT TRANSPOSING DEVICE)

£28 net.

COME AND SEE IT AT ONCE

METZLER & CO., LIMITED

42 GREAT MARLBOROUGH ST., LONDON, W.

WHAT IS A STEEL BARLESS GRAND?

AN EMINENT ENGINEER WRITES:

Stisted Hall,
Braintree,
October 12th, 1903.

Gentlemen,

I am glad to tell you that I am very pleased with the Instrument, and my musical friends admire it very much.

The tone is remarkably rich, full, and brilliant, and at the same time sweet and mellow—whilst the touch is most delicate and the workmanship is all I could desire. I consider the barless frame to be quite a triumph in engineering. In working out the tensile strength upon the whole of the wires, I find the total strain must be nearly 25 tons, yet the frame is so beautifully proportioned, the metal being distributed exactly where it is most wanted, that when the wires are slackened and the whole of the heavy strain released, there is no permanent set in the frame, but it goes back to its original shape. The advantage of this is very great, since all the wires are kept constantly at the necessary tension for giving the right pitch to each note. The old method of having iron frames with stiffening bars above the wires is unquestionably at a disadvantage, whereas with your barless frame the notes are extremely clear and brilliant.

I am, yours faithfully,

(Signed) JAMES PAXMAN.

Messrs. John Broadwood & Sons, Ltd.

JOHN BROADWOOD & SONS, Ltd.
35, GREAT PULTENEY STREET, LONDON, W.
(Close to Piccadilly Circus).

THE METROSTYLE PIANOLA

As well as providing correct technique and enabling any one to play the piano, this instrument indicates interpretation.

As most people know, music for the Pianola takes the form of perforated paper rolls, and in the case of the Metrostyle Pianola these rolls have been played over by great musicians and are marked by them with a red line showing the interpretation. Any one who possesses a Metrostyle Pianola can reproduce the artist's playing with all the changes of tempo, the phrasing, and dynamic effects.

Paderewski, Bauer, Hofmann, Moszkowski, Chaminade, Strauss, Grieg, &c., have all interpreted compositions for the Metrostyle Pianola.

A few months ago Sir Edward Elgar called at Æolian Hall to investigate the Pianola, and was so interested in the instrument that he specially interpreted several of his own compositions, so that Metrostyle owners might be enabled to render them in the way he considers they should be played.

It is conclusive proof of the artistic excellence of the Metrostyle Pianola that famous pianists and composers should identify themselves so closely with it. It would interest you to call and see it. Specify Catalogue S. when writing for particulars.

THE ORCHESTRELLE COMPANY
ÆOLIAN HALL
135-6-7 NEW BOND ST., LONDON, W.

LIVING MASTERS
OF MUSIC

AN ILLUSTRATED SERIES OF
MONOGRAPHS DEALING WITH
CONTEMPORARY MUSICAL LIFE
& INCLUDING REPRESENTATIVES
OF ALL BRANCHES OF THE ART

EDITED BY
ROSA NEWMARCH.

EDITOR'S NOTE.

IT seems evident that the years are bringing back to the Anglo-Saxon races that wider and more social interest in music which, half a century ago, seems to have dwindled to a languid, dilettante patronage of Italian Opera. Every year a larger number of the public become habitual concert-goers, and music seems to be entering upon a healthier and more democratic phase of its existence. With this revived interest comes a desire to know something more of the master-spirits of the musical world; not merely of the old classical composers, but of those living personalities who are actually shaping the destinies of the art.

EDITOR'S NOTE (Continued).

Biographies of Bach, Handel, and Mendelssohn, for all their instructive value, tell us nothing of the present day. The men who are making history in politics, warfare, or science have a strong grip on our interests and imaginations. Judging from the success of many recent memoirs, and the increasing number of series devoted to books on living celebrities, it seems as though contemporary biography, with its glow and actuality, exercised an endless fascination for the public. As far as I am aware, no English or American series has attempted to do for musicians what has been done for living men of letters, soldiers, statesmen, or scientists. It is to be hoped that the "Living Masters of Music" series will supply this deficiency by giving the public just those details about the composers and executive artists whom they hear and see, as will enable them to realise their individual influence on contemporary music.

The scope of these volumes is wider than that of any other musical series now before the British or American public, since it is intended to include representatives of every branch of musical activity, provided they are really central figures in their own sphere. The interpreting conductor—that latest phenomenon in the world of music—the *virtuoso*, the master-teacher—possibly even the great vocalist—will be represented in these volumes as well as the creative artist.

The distinguishing feature of the books will be that touch of intimacy which gives to contemporary biography its greatest value and vitality. As far as possible, each volume will be confided to a writer who is actually acquainted with the personality and the work of the musician he is invited to depict. We are confident that such a series will have more interest for the musical public than those which deal exclusively with composers of the past. Biographical matter will not be neglected, but each book will aim at being an essay on the man and his work, rather than a detailed biography. In the case of composers, the volumes will contain a complete list of works up to date, portraits, fac-similes, and other illustrations.

JOHN LANE, Publisher, London and New York.

A BOOK OF OLD-FASHIONED MUSIC

OLD ENGLISH
SONGS & DANCES

BY

W. GRAHAM ROBERTSON

With 46 Illustrations in Colour by
the Author.   Large Folio

Price 21s. net

*A special feature of this work is the coloured
Illustrations, reproduced by means of
wood-blocks engraved and printed
by Mr. Edmund Evans, at
the Racquet Court Press*

JOHN LANE, Publisher, LONDON & NEW YORK